TALKING
TOTEM POLES

TALKING TOTEM POLES

Glenn Holder

Illustrated with Photographs and a Map

DODD, MEAD & COMPANY
New York

FRONTISPIECE: *Totem at Thunderbird Park, Victoria, British Columbia*

ACKNOWLEDGMENTS

For either information or pictorial assistance, the author is especially indebted to the Alaska State Museum; Norman J. Boudreau of the National Museum of Canada; Helen Byrd of the Richmond, Indiana, Public Schools; the Canadian Government Travel Bureau; Thomas Y. Crowell Company; Department of Travel of British Columbia; Viola E. Garfield of the University of Washington; Alice Hoover of the Ball State University Library; the Maywood Avenue Elementary School, Maywood, New Jersey; Juanita B. Pike of the University of Washington Press; the James C. Ryan Junior High School, Fairbanks, Alaska; the Provincial Archives, Victoria, British Columbia; the Smithsonian Institution; State of Alaska Travel Division; Superior Publishing Company of Seattle; United States Forest Service and Allan Taylor; and Western Airlines. Many others generously helped, too, in one way or another.

The legend of the Giant Rock Oyster pole in Chapter IV is quoted verbatim, by permission, from the book *The Wolf and the Raven: Totem Poles of Southeastern Alaska* by Viola E. Garfield and Linn A. Forrest.

MAP on page 11 by Salem Tamer.

PHOTOGRAPHS courtesy of:
Alaska Travel Division: 46; British Columbia Government Photograph: frontispiece, 8 left and center, 18 left, 32, 35, 36, 38; Canadian Government Travel Bureau Photo: 24, 26, 27 top, 37, 42, 62, 75 left; Charles L. Clutts: 71; Patrick Ferro: 72, 73; Geological Survey of Canada: 41; Glenbow-Alberta Institute Photograph: 27 bottom; Metropolitan Life Insurance Company: 75 right; Museum of the American Indian, Heye Foundation: 18 right, 30 top right, 52 top, 55; National Musuem of Canada: 8 right; Provincial Archives, Victoria, B. C.: 56, 58, 59; United States Forest Service: 12, 14, 15 (Allan Taylor), 16, 23, 30 bottom, 34, 39 (Allan Taylor), 48 left, 50, 52 bottom, 61, 64, 66, 68, 76; University of Washington Press: 48 right; Western Airlines Photo: 21, 30 top left, 33, 40, 45.

To Helen, my wife, whose idea it was that
we visit totemland and explore its wonders

Contents

1
What Is a Totem Pole?

THE TOTEM POLE of the Northwestern Coast Indians was a sign-board. Carved with both animal and human figures, the pole was a substitute for the printed word, something these Indians had not invented. The totem pole showed the history of a man, his clan, or family, especially any victories in war and other favorable things that had happened.

The carver of the pole took special care to reveal anything mysterious that had happened to the tribe, such as stories or myths from the long ago. Using the carved pole, a man could say whatever he wanted to say, and his family, friends, and neighbors could understand. The totem pole was as necessary to these Indians as were their stone bowls for grinding grain, stone-tipped lances for spearing fish, bows for hunting, and flintheads for tipping arrows.

The totem pole was never something to be worshiped, nor had it any religious meaning. Neither did the poles have anything to do with the practice of witchcraft. The red cedar figures on the poles told the life story of the Indians, no more, no less.

Totem poles are found only in northwestern North America. Why, it is wondered, didn't people elsewhere in the world make them? Of course, carvings similar in many ways to totem poles

Haida poles, (Left) at Prince Rupert, others at Thunderbird Park, British Columbia

9

were done in other parts of the world. The Maoris of New Zealand did excellent wood carving, but their work was mainly in the decorating of houses, canoes, and smaller items. The Maoris were fond of carving the human face on house posts and rafters, but nothing so large and complicated as a sixty-foot totem pole was ever attempted by them.

Other peoples carved in stone instead of wood, including the early Greek and Roman sculptors, and the Easter Islanders of the South Pacific who made strange-looking figures with large heads.

But totem poles were made only from Puget Sound to approximately two hundred miles northwest of Juneau, Alaska. This area was a thousand miles long and in places as much as a hundred miles wide. Totemland included the Alaska Panhandle, so called because on the map it resembles the handle of a cooking pan, and the nearby areas of British Columbia. Nearly all of this part of Alaska and British Columbia is heavily timbered with red cedar, spruce, hemlock, pine, and cottonwood. The totem nations in Alaska were the Tlingit, Haida, Kwakiutl, and the Nootka. The Quilliute and Coast Salish nations were in the states of Washington and Oregon, and the Tsimsyan and Bella Coola nations were in British Columbia. Each nation was divided into tribes, the tribes into clans, and the clans into closely related families.

European explorers first reported seeing totem poles in Alaska in the late 1700's. Totems probably existed earlier than that. Most experts agree that totem-pole carving is a little more than three hundred years old. The Haidas seem to have made the first poles, the idea being borrowed later by other tribes. Stories that have been handed down say that the very first totem pole floated in from the sea.

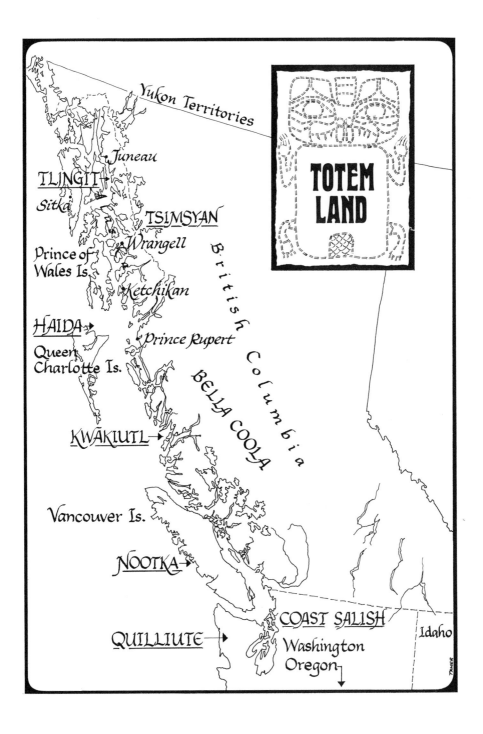

Yukon Territories

TOTEM
LAND

Juneau

TLINGIT

Sitka

TSIMSYAN

Wrangell

Prince of
Wales Is.

Ketchikan

British Columbia

HAIDA

Prince Rupert

Queen
Charlotte Is.

BELLA COOLA

KWAKIUTL

Vancouver Is.

NOOTKA

COAST SALISH

Idaho

QUILLIUTE

Washington
Oregon

Bears and ravens (Tlingit) guard the entrances
to Saxman Park near Ketchikan, Alaska.

Explorer George Vancouver of England, for whom a city in Canada is named, described the totem poles he found when he visited the Northwest Coast from 1793 to 1794. "Here," he said, "were erected two pillars sixteen feet high and four feet in circumference, painted white; on top of each was placed a large square box; on examining one of them, it was found to contain many ashes and pieces of burnt bones, which were considered to be human; these relics were carefully wrapped up in skins and old mats, and at the base of the pillars was placed an old canoe in which there were some paddles." The poles seen by Vancouver, probably none of which exist today, were small and rudely carved because they had been done with simple, crude tools. The most artistic and largest poles were to be made many years later when the iron tools brought by the white man were used.

Don Alexandro Malaspina, an Italian explorer, gave another early account of the poles. "We do not know," he explained in describing a large bear totem, "whether the colossal monster which occupies the foreground is an idol or merely a frightful record of the destructive nature of death. . . . In a casket which lay beneath its claws or hands was a bowl-shaped basket, a European hat, an otter skin and a piece of board. The height of the monster was no less than ten and a half feet."

No one can say for certain just how it happened that the totem form of art came to this particular part of the world. Some people have an idea that the land, sea, and weather had much to do with it. The place where the totem poles were made was a land of plenty, with cool summers and long and usually mild and rainy winters. Fish were plentiful in the sea and streams, and they were easily caught by hand or with simple tools. Wild game for clothing and food was also abundant, along with fruits,

The carving of totem poles developed in a land of forests and water. This view is of the site of an Indian village, now abandoned. Once there were many totems here (see page 68).

roots, and berries. It was much easier to find food and shelter here than it was in many other parts of the world. Since the making of a living was not a full-time job for the Indians, some of them turned to the arts. One of these arts was the carving of totem poles by a few skilled members of the tribe.

Each totem pole was different, and each carver tried to outdo his neighbor in cutting skill, beauty, arrangement, and originality. No carver wanted to be a copycat.

There was one weakness in the poles. Made of wood and left standing outside, in time they gave way to weather and insects, lasting only about fifty to sixty years. Furthermore, once a pole had been raised, usually with great ceremony, nothing was done to protect it. Owners let their poles rot and sink into the earth.

Most of the old totem poles rotted and fell down because their owners did nothing to preserve the wood.

United States forester surveys restored Tlingit poles at Klawock Totem Park near Wrangell, Alaska. Note the plants growing out of the hollow back of hawk in the second pole, foreground.

Since most poles would last one man's lifetime, that seemed to be long enough to the Indians. A totem pole was a personal thing, and a son usually did not have much interest in the totem of his father, grandfather, or any other ancestor. The son wanted a new pole, one of his very own. Then, too, any work in saving the pole was expensive, because this called for another ceremony. So most of the old totems were lost.

Since the higher the totem the greater the recognition of its owner, feuds often broke out when the chiefs struggled to outdo each other. One of the best known of these quarrels was between Hladerh and Sispegut, both of the Gitksan tribe of the Tsimsyan nation. Hladerh, chief of the Wolf clan, was the proud owner of the tallest totem pole in the area. When Chief Sispegut of the Finback Whales clan announced that he had plans to erect the tallest pole in the vicinity, Hladerh angrily warned Sispegut that this would not be allowed. Sispegut had the taller pole carved anyway. Hladerh answered Sispegut by shooting him, wounding him seriously, as Sispegut rode by in a canoe.

The feud was not to end there. Later, through a plot, Hladerh had a nephew of Sispegut murder his uncle.

Hladerh also humiliated a chief of his own tribe by forcing him to shorten a pole after it had been erected. When the other chief did shorten his pole, Hladerh was still unhappy because, he said, the pole was still too tall. So he forced the chief to cut off several feet more.

The totem pole, then, was a monument, an emblem of a strong and loyal people. The ways of life that made the poles have vanished, but some of the art still endures.

The job of the carver was to tell a story. Each figure was a symbol.

The totem Indians began by carving masks. This one of a hawk (decorated with ermine skins) was made by the Kwakiutl nation.

II
Carving the Totem Pole

THE CARVING of large numbers of totem poles began about 1820. During the fifty years that followed, the best totem work was done by the Tsimsyan, Tlingit, and Haida nations.

The making of totem poles is thought to have come from a custom certain tribes had of carving small, simple figures, called crest figures, of animals or persons on tombstones and house fronts. Or totem-pole making could have developed from the carving of other small figures in the form of masks worn by actors in festivals. Usually painted yellow, orange, or red, these masks designated the tribe of the Indians who wore them.

Artists today paint, carve, chisel, or compose according to their own choices and imaginations, but totem-pole carvers had no such freedom. An Indian totem artist worked entirely from directions supplied by the chief who had hired him, just as a modern-day house builder follows an architect's blueprint. Nor did the carver select the red cedar tree to be used, the spot where the finished pole would be set, or the number or kind of figures that would appear on the pole. Even though he had great talent, the carver always did exactly what the owner told him to do.

The carver had to remember that his first job was to make the pole tell a story, and tell it well. The appearance of the pole was

19

secondary. Then there were certain national, tribal, and even family customs that had to be followed in the making of each pole. But in spite of all the rules and restrictions under which they worked, certain carvers did manage to make beautiful and original poles. Somehow, too, each pole showed the personal touch of the man who carved it; no one else could make a pole exactly like his.

The schooling of a carver, often like the training given artists today, began in early childhood. If a youth seemed to have promising artistic talents, he was taught the meanings of the clan's spirits and the wisdom of the medicine man. He also learned the history, ceremonies, songs, and secrets of the tribe, and entered its high councils. All the while he studied under an expert carver, and his training lasted until he came of age. Only a few youths in each tribe were fortunate enough to become apprentices. Even fewer became skilled workmen.

When a chief decided he was wealthy enough to own a totem pole, he began the search for a carver. This chiseler of wood was chosen carefully; his reputation as a carver had to be of the best. A chief might reject many carvers before he selected one he felt could do the work exactly as he wanted it done.

Carvers known for their excellent work were in short supply. Pole customers often had to wait many months, perhaps for as long as a year, before their poles could be started. The services of good carvers were expensive, too, some charging a sum that today would amount to a thousand dollars. The best carvers often went great distances to make the poles, and because they traveled from tribe to tribe, the poles of the various nations

Today only a few Indians are being taught to carve totem poles. These are at Port Chilkoot, Alaska. Note carved masks on Indian boys in background.

Trunk of a red cedar tree, favored by carvers of totem poles

This stump of a red cedar tree gives some idea of the tremendous job it was for early Indians with primitive tools to cut one down, move it, and carve it.

This old pole is in the Kitmancool Lake District of British Columbia. The hollowed out back shows clearly.

grow, had to tow these trees great distances, sometimes through stormy waters. The northern carvers often used the large cotton-wood tree that grew in their country. But the cottonwood was harder to carve and did not last nearly so long as the red cedar, and so was a poor substitute.

Before the white man traded steel tools to the Indians for sea otter furs and other goods, the carvers had only simple dull knives and chisels made of stone, bone, wood, or, in rare cases, copper. With sharper and sturdier iron tools, especially the adze and the curved knife, the carver was able to turn out better poles with less effort.

Apprentices or helpers usually did much of the early rough work on the pole, such as marking the trunk into sections and chipping away certain parts of the wood. But the faces and limbs of the figures called for the careful hand of the experienced master craftsman. The back side of the pole, the hollowed-out part, was not decorated with figures, and neither was the part of the pole that would be placed in the ground.

To decorate the poles—and to preserve them as much as they could—the Indians used bright paints made of animal oils and blood, salmon eggs, charcoal, graphite, ocher, and moss. Paint brushes were made of animal fur. The decorating of the poles was so important that the master carver himself usually did that work, although apprentices helped in collecting the materials that went into the paint. One tribe, the Bella Bellas of the Kwakiutl nation of Alaska, became so skillful and busy in the making of the color mixture and in applying it that they left the carving to artists in other tribes and "specialized." The native paints, however, did very little to preserve the poles, the sun soon fading the colors and the rain washing them away.

Among the groups of carvers there were none that did their

work more expertly than the Tsimsyan *gitsontk*—people who work by themselves. They were the best trained of all. Like other artists, they tried to carve in complete secrecy, but the *gitsontk* killed anyone caught spying on them at work. A *gitsontk* himself could also be put to death were he to make a serious mistake in any way when carving.

To show their skill further, a group of *gitsontk* once made a wooden boat in the shape of a whale. The craft was large enough

This painted face was carved in the late 1880's.

Whales were popular subjects for totem poles. (Below) War chief of Chilcat Indians with family in front of two horizontal crest figures of killer whales (1885); (Left) restored pole shows attack of Thunderbird on a whale.

to carry several strong fighters. Its purpose was to frighten an enemy, who might consider it an evil spirit. But on a trial run, with many people looking on, the boat went out of control. Knowing that he would be put to death for his failure, the head *gitsontk* drowned himself on the spot. The crew members were not seen again.

Totem-pole sculpture was the work of a number of gifted persons, only a few of whom are known by name.

One of the great carvers recorded in history was Haesem-hliyawn of the Gitksan tribe of the Tsimsyan nation. He probably made the best human figures anywhere. His carvings show true facial expressions—sadness, seriousness, happiness. He was equally skilled in the making of birds and other figures. It was during the years 1840 to 1880, the time of greatest interest in the poles, that Haesem did his work. Some of his poles may still be seen.

Two other well-known carvers remembered by name were Arthur Moody of the Haidas and Paul Jones of the Tlingits. They did their best work with miniature totems. These poles varied from about four to twenty-four inches in height, although very few of the short ones were made. The miniature poles were sold in great numbers to visitors from outside of totemland.

The greatest of all the Indian artists was Charlie Edensaw, a Haida of the Queen Charlotte Islands. He carved during most of his eighty-five years (1839-1924). Actually, Edensaw called himself a silversmith, since he did much of his work in that medium. But he also did beautiful work in wood and in a type of soft rock called argellite. His art did not include the large totems, but he did carve many beautiful miniature poles from yew wood. He was the third in a line of three generations of Edensaws, all carvers. However, Charlie surpassed in skill both his father, a canoemaker, and his grandfather, a copper-shield craftsman.

Faced with the new ways of life that the white man had brought, the totem-pole Indians gradually lost interest in the wood sculpture that once had meant so much to them. With their work no longer in demand at the beginning of the new century, the master carvers soon became a part of the dim past.

But in recent years the memory of the old sculptors is being recalled by a new generation of Americans and Canadians who see in the old totem poles a great contribution to the world's art. So, after being long neglected, the carvers of red cedar are beginning to receive deserved recognition.

Tlingit house pillar entrance (Left), Chief Shakes Community House at Wrangell, Alaska. (Right) Tlingit wolf house post (1905). The roof beam fitted into the notched top.

House posts lasted longer because they were indoors. The carving shows on two poles in this abandoned Haida house at Old Kasaan, Prince of Wales Island, which is being inspected by United States foresters.

III
Kinds of Totem Poles

THE Northwest Coast Indians made six main kinds of totem poles or posts, all calling attention to what had happened in the past. These included the *house pillar* or *false house pillar,* the *mortuary* or *funeral,* the *memorial,* the *heraldic portal,* the *welcoming,* and the *shame* poles. Each type was a different kind of reminder. There were only a few poles that did not fit into one of these six classes.

The *house pillars,* which seem to have been the earliest totems made, served first of all as supports for the building beams. It was an easy matter to carve the totem figures on the smooth surfaces of these posts.

Four carved pillars were used by the Haidas to hold up the beams of their large public houses. In some cases the story that a carving told was continued from one pole to another. These totems were also often decorated with shells, ermine, or human hair.

The Tlingits did not carve directly on the house post. They cut the totem on another piece of red cedar, and then attached it to the house post. This carving became a false part of the house pillar. Sometimes there were as many as eight of these totems in one building. The Tlingit custom was a good one because their carvings could easily be removed if the owner wished

to place them in another house, or if they were threatened by fire, floods, or other dangers. The totem was never sold by one Indian to another because no one had any interest in another's family history.

When an Indian was about to begin an important task, custom required him to go without food and water for the number of days equal to the total totem pillars in his home. This fasting was believed to make the man humble, thus causing him to take his work more seriously. The wealthy suffered much in doing important tasks because some of their homes had as many as eight pillars. More of the house-post carvings remain today than any of the other types because these pillars were indoors and were thus protected from the damp weather common in that part of the world.

The *mortuary* or *funeral* pole, raised in respect to the dead, was a tomb marker. The body of the dead person was cremated and the ashes were then placed in a box on the top of the pole.

(Left) Grave figure carved by Bella Coola Indians

Two Tlingit mortuary totems, the Sea Serpent and the Bear Up Mountain, at Wrangell

The first mortuary poles, probably dating back many centuries, had no totem carvings, but the plain poles were sometimes painted. At a later time, perhaps near the end of the 1700's, a carved wooden figure, often that of a bear, was attached to the top of the pole, and the ashes of the dead were placed in a hole in the ground at the back of the pole.

Later mortuary-pole makers began to add carvings that told the main events of the dead person's life. It was in this way that the totem Indians showed their deep respect for the departed members of the family and tribe. The pole was placed among the other mortuary poles of the family in a tribal burying ground. Burial spots were near the tribal dwellings. But mortuary poles were used less and less as the missionaries, who began to arrive in small numbers in the early 1800's, taught Christian burial.

Mortuary totems in the Haida tribal burying ground at Old Kasaan

Tsimsyan memorial pole

The *memorial* pole, considered by the Indians to be the most important of all, had a number of special uses. It could honor a dead chief, show the family claim of the new chief to the tribal leadership, or tell other important facts about the chief's family. Custom required that the memorial pole be carved and erected at the order of the new chief, but only after he had served as leader for a year. Thus memorials for dead chiefs were delayed. The totems raised at potlatches were memorial poles in most cases.

Because the memorial pole was the most important totem of all, the Indians searched for the tallest, strongest, straightest, and most beautifully formed red cedar when they began to fashion this type of totem. Many of these poles stood fifty feet high

when finished, and a few reached eighty feet. Such high totems usually had carvings only at the top and bottom. Shorter, thicker memorial poles were usually decorated with carvings from top to bottom.

Though such poles in most cases honored the dead chief and the present chief, it was not at all uncommon for the wife of the new chief to be included also. In some tribes the totem of the wife was placed at the top of the pole. Other tribes carved the wife's totem lower down.

The *heraldic portal* or family pole, which was placed in the front of a dwelling, told of the great importance of the people who lived there. Any failures or unhappiness the family had known were not, of course, included on the totem.

Entrance to the house was through a wide hole in the totem crest. European explorers first saw an example of this type of pole on Langara Island, one of the Queen Charlotte group, in 1790. The Langara totem, a rather simple one, was short and broad. Heraldic poles made later were larger and more ornate and thus harder to make than the Langara totem.

36

The heraldic portal pole told of the family and gave entrance to the house. (Left) Bella Coola pole, restored; (Right) Tsimsyan pole.

Two welcoming poles (Nootka) in Thunderbird Park

(Right) A former resident of Old Kasaan stares at the charred remains of one of two welcoming poles. The house he lived in as a boy was just behind this pole.

The *welcoming* pole of the waterfront owner greeted guests and marked off a section of the ocean front or river beach for a chief.

Though serving good purposes, the welcoming poles were not as important as the other kinds. Usually found in pairs, the welcoming totems showed that the space between the poles was the chief's personal property and that it was not owned by the tribe. But the welcoming poles were meant only for invited guests, uninvited persons being treated rudely or even roughly if they came to this part of the waterfront.

Carrying only a few symbols, the welcoming poles were made by young men learning under the masters. It was seldom that these poles were even painted. Most of these totems were made by the Nootkas who lived on Vancouver Island and nearby. For some unknown reason, this kind of pole was not popular with the northern nations.

The upside-down figure below the bear, dogfish, and wolf on this memorial pole to Chief Ebbits of Tongass signifies a debt owed to the chief.

(Right) Many totems appear in this photograph of a Haida village at Skedans, Queen Charlotte Islands.

The *shame* pole was used mainly by chiefs to force the payment of debts. With the story of failure carved for all to see, debts were often paid promptly. One way to shame a man with unpaid debts was to carve his totem upside down. Indian chiefs seldom used this type of pole on their fellow chiefs. There usually was a serious attempt to solve debt problems between chiefs in some other way. But white explorers and colonists owing debts to Indians often appeared on this type of totem. With outsiders there was no need to be easy. In a few cases the shame totem told of some scandal, and, as in the case of debt, outsiders were more often subjects than Indians.

Special totems showing threat, anger, or revenge also were carved, but in small numbers. They were somewhat like the shame poles in purpose, but they dealt with more serious matters like murder, kidnapping, robbery, or the counterfeiting of copper money. These poles served as a kind of law court, the totem punishing the guilty person by holding him up for public disgrace. This type of totem may have decreased the number of crimes, but its erection often brought with it quarrels, fights, and sometimes tribal wars. An Indian chief thought long and carefully before he raised this special pole. He needed to be certain, absolutely certain, that the subject was guilty of the crime before ridiculing him.

Totem Glade in Vancouver's Stanley Park shows the adeptness of Canada's Pacific Coast Indians as totem-pole carvers.

IV
What a Totem Pole Says

TOTEM POLES were not really "read," because the symbols used on them were of no help if the passerby did not already know the story. Rather the items on the poles served as reminders. A totem pole is like a poem in that it hints at a great deal more than it actually says.

The complete story of the symbols on a pole was known only to those who had heard the speeches and songs and had seen the dances at the pole raising. One pole might deal with a short tale, a long one, or a series of tales. The stories began at the top of the pole and extended downward. Contrary to the general belief today, it was not always uncomplimentary for an Indian to be the "low man on the totem pole." That is, the arrangement from top to bottom was sometimes based on things other than importance or rank.

Of the more than one hundred symbols carved on poles, some were used more than others, the tribes often choosing animals to identify themselves. Bird symbols were quite popular. Portraying evil, the serpent or snake symbol appeared on many poles in the southern part of totemland. Shown with two heads, the snake could shed his scales and make lightning when attacked. The halibut and frog symbols, easily recognized because they were usually carved to look like real animals, were common. Also often seen and easily identified was the beaver with his large teeth, paddle-like tail, and a stick in his front paws.

Other symbols frequently used were the bear, killer whale, seal, thunderbird, and the woodworm (considered a type of dragon). Included less often were the owl, eagle, hawk, cormorant, crane, woodpecker, loon, starfish, sea lion, shark, bullhead, land otter, groundhog, mountain goat, and puma. In a few cases, the moon and stars were used as symbols, as were rainbows, sea monsters, mosquitoes, dragonflies, and butterflies.

Whole figures were often represented in various ways in the limited space of a pole. A fin or fluted tail stood for a fish or sea animal, a wing for a bird, and a claw, snout, or sharp teeth for a bear or wolf.

The entire human body was sometimes represented by a face. Wings attached to a symbol suggested the ability to fly, the ear meant hearing and understanding, and the eye was the power of life. To save even more space, birds, beavers, and humans were carved with their limbs close to their bodies, and in some cases the symbol was upside down. Often one figure overlapped the symbols above or below it. Other strange positions were often necessary in order to fit the symbols into the limited space.

When the carver had space to spare, something that didn't happen very often, he used fins, bird tails, or feathers as decorations. They were mere fillers, not adding to the story. It was always necessary that the carver put as much of the story or stories as possible on the pole.

Fortunately, most of the old totem poles can be interpreted in some way today. The stories their symbols tell have been carried down through several generations. The few poles whose stories have been lost are called puzzle totems.

Some totems are very well known, one of the best being the

A puzzle totem—no one knows the story of this pole, although the salmon symbol can be seen at the bottom.

Sun and Raven pole carved in 1902 by the Tlingits. Now standing in Saxman Totem Park, near Ketchikan, Alaska, this carving reminds viewers of three adventures of Raven, the folk hero. His wings outspread and his head enclosed in a sun halo, Raven appears at the top of the pole. This first of the three stories tells of the birth of Raven. Decorating his breast are the three chil-

dren of the Sun, who were visited by Raven when floods covered the earth. In placing raven tracks on the face of the female figure, the carver was following the custom among women of the Raven clan.

On Raven's wings are eyes containing small faces, a reminder that he could change form when he wished to do so. The other carvings on this top part of the pole are feathers, which are mere decorations.

The second Raven story on the pole shows the face of Daughter of the Fog, or Fog Woman, above the head of Raven which appears again nearer the bottom of the pole, and six salmon, three on each side of Raven.

The third Raven story continues on the lower part of the pole, as Raven dives toward Frog. There are small faces on Frog's feet. In the story, Frog carries Raven to the bottom of the sea after the floods which had covered the earth have subsided. They saw many strange sights on the journey, but the pole does not suggest any of them.

It was the symbol of Raven that attracted the most attention from the totem-pole carvers. Raven, that amazing bird, had brought light into the world and had made the rivers, lakes, and ocean. He could change himself handily into a man, woman, or anything else whenever he wished. He is always shown with a straight beak to set him apart from other birds. The straight beak was still used even when Raven turned himself into a combined bird and human being, which he often did in the stories. The hawk was shown with a large curving beak, the point hooked back, while the eagle's beak was pointed downward.

The Tired Wolf house post, carved about 1827, tells the story

Sun and Raven pole, carved in 1902, tells three stories about Raven.

47

(Right) Loon Tree pole

(Below) Tired Wolf pole. As totem artists often did, this carver showed a whole face in the eye.

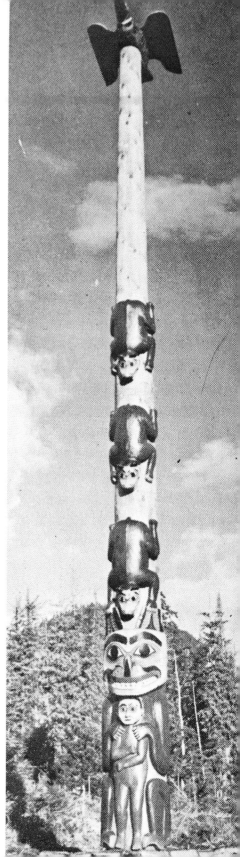

of a wolf that was a friend of man. This post is now located in Saxman Park. Another Tired Wolf house post may also be seen at Saxman Park. However, the first mentioned is considered the better of the two because it shows the left eye as a face. The carving is different from those of most totem animal figures because it does not face forward or downward on the post but sideways.

The Loon Tree totem pole reminds the passerby of what happened long ago to the forefathers of the Kats House of the Tongass tribe of the Tlingit nation, who lived not far from the present town of Wrangell. This pole, which is also at Saxman Park, is a copy of one brought from Cape Fox Village. Four carvers, three of whom were of the Tlingit nation and one of the Haida, made the new pole. At the top of the pole sits the loon followed by three bear cubs pointing down. At the bottom of the pole is the bear wife with her husband, Kats, in her arms.

The Giant Rock Oyster pole, also at Saxman Park, is a mortuary totem. The family ties of the four divisions of the Nexadi clan of the Tlingits are shown, starting with the Eagle Claw House carving at the top of the pole. The beaver, which comes next, stands for the Beaver House part of the family, and the second beaver means the Beaver Tail House division. The face at the bottom of the pole refers to the Giant Rock Oyster House family, which took its name from the following legend:

"Many years ago there was a Tlingit village at Kasaan Bay. One day several men went to a reef at the north end of the village at low tide to hunt devilfish. Soon a young man located one of them under a rock. Taking his long-handled hook, he poked it into the hiding place and hooked the fish, but it tore loose and moved out of reach. The man dug around the rock with a stick and finally put his hand into the crevice, though his companions

49

Giant Rock
Oyster pole

cautioned him against it. As he reached under the rock, a giant rock oyster caught him by the wrist.

"His companions could not extricate him, so they sent to the village for help. They tried to pry the oyster open, but the shells only closed more tightly. The boulder was too heavy to lift, and the efforts to turn it over failed. It only sank deeper into the sand, pinning the unfortunate victim beneath it. As they frantically worked to free him, the tide rose higher and higher. When it reached the victim's shoulders, he began to sing:

'Where is the tide, where is the tide?
Watch for thyself, watch for thyself.
Oh, spirits of tide, they are coming up.
Oh, spirits of tide, they are coming up.
Oh, sons of tide spirit, they are coming up.'

"The tide reached his shoulders, but the imprisoned man continued to sing. The water covered him completely, and he was dead.

"When the tide fell, his relatives found his body on the beach. The giant oyster had let him go. The song he composed was sung at his funeral, and since that time it has been owned by his descendants. They also took Giant Rock Oyster as the name for their house."

Tlingit dugout on shore near Sitka, Alaska. The canoe was the means of travel in this area.

Dotted line indicates area of the Haida village at Old Kasaan, the scene of many a potlatch. An earlier Tlingit village may have occupied this site, "Kasaan" being a Tlingit word meaning "place of pretty village." In this photo, only one totem pole remains, as the forest reclaims its own.

V
The Potlatch

THE POTLATCH was an important and festive gathering of tribes
to dedicate and explain a new totem pole. It was a time for gift-
giving and for telling of plans for the future. It was also a time
for honoring members of the tribe who has done good deeds.
The Indians liked to pay debts at the potlatch, too, because
those present could provide proof, if needed, that the debts had
been paid. As allowed by tribal law, the host chief could explain
his family history at the potlatch. This was done best by the
totem pole, the nearest thing these Indians had to a written
language. White explorers thought the potlatch was a time only
for showing off belongings and for drinking and wild celebra-
tion. They did not understand the real purpose of the event.

Potlatch crowds varied in size. The smallest ones included
only the closely related members of a clan. The largest meetings
also included clans distantly related, some of whom lived as far
away as a hundred miles. But in the area, travel was fairly easy
by canoe on the ocean, the hundreds of ocean inlets, and the
many rivers and smaller streams.

When a chief felt he had enough wealth to hold a potlatch,
he first considered whom he should invite. Not just anybody
would do. Often he sent his friends or servants out to notify
guests of the coming potlatch. They would be told later of the

exact time of the event. A good guest was one from whom the chief himself could expect to receive the most benefit. That is, the host needed guests who would be willing and able to accept the presents he gave them and then, later, to repay him with even more valuable gifts. A man who had a poor reputation for paying his debts had little chance of receiving invitations to the great feasts.

The preparations for the potlatch required the help of all the members of the host chief's family, including his wife, children, brothers, sisters, grandparents, uncles, aunts, and cousins. Not the least important task was the gathering and storing of large amounts of prepared and unprepared food. The guests were always hungry when they arrived, and they would have to be fed well during the several days of the potlatch, too. But the collection of food was usually easy since wildlife was plentiful, and the streams and ocean contained many fish. Berries, nuts, and roots could be found in large amounts in the forest during the short summer. The food, often in dried form, was stored in the houses or in other protected places. Gifts consisting of blankets, clothing, tools, weapons, copper shields, and other articles had to be collected.

To make certain that everything was ready, the chief used a group of inspectors, a kind of committee, to check on whether the potlatch preparations really were in order. A poorly planned potlatch brought only trouble, not profit, to the host. Any shortage of food and proper gifts would anger the guests and cause them to punish the chief in various ways later. So only when the committee of experts had decided everything was ready were messengers sent to summon the chosen visitors, sometimes as many as a hundred.

The guests usually traveled to the potlatch in canoes deco-

Wooden carvings (Kwakiutl) represent men holding copper shields, or "coppers," which were valuable potlatch gifts.

Guests usually paddled a long way to a potlatch. (Photo was taken in 1887 of Tlingit Indians.)

On the way, guests stopped to dress up before proceeding to the potlatch. (This photo, taken in 1914, is actually of a Kwakiutl wedding party. Note carving on canoe.)

rated with crests showing their family coat-of-arms and carrying cooking equipment, extra clothing, and other articles necessary for the trip. In the early days the canoes were paddled by slaves, the honored guests not doing that kind of labor. The canoes were halted at some distance from the host's beach so that the guests could ready themselves for a grand entrance. The preparations included the painting of faces and changing to clothing made especially for the event. Seldom were there late arrivals to a potlatch. Being tardy was considered bad taste.

When everything was ready, the guests, singing a song of peace, began to row toward the host's house. The chief and the members of his family, facing the oncoming guests, answered with another song. Dancing by both groups followed, and then the guests were presented to the host by a master of ceremonies.

The introductions over, it was time for the feast, which consisted of boiled or roasted meat, fish, soup, and berry cakes. During the feast came speeches by the host and others he had chosen. The invited orators always spoke well of the host and his tribe and clan, found fault with his enemies, and praised the guests. Then, with the feast continuing, there was time for conversation, storytelling, games, and visiting. As the campfires blazed, the talk continued far into the night, and into the following several days until the potlatch ended. The guests slept late each morning. There was no need to hurry while attending a potlatch.

The most important visitors slept in the chief's house. Other guests slept outside, usually beneath canoes turned upside down.

Each day presents were given by the host, with the guests of high rank receiving the most costly ones. The problem of the value of a gift was troublesome. It was in as poor taste to present a gift of small value as to give one of too great a value.

A gift of small value meant that the host felt the receiver had little ability or desire to pay his potlatch debts. This situation often caused the receiver to feel insulted. A gift of great value sometimes made demands on a guest that were out of line with his wealth or willingness to repay. Since the wrong gifts could mean trouble, even among the tribes, potlatch presents called for careful handling. The giving and receiving of gifts was an important part of the business life of a tribe. Actually, it was a system of trade, articles not needed being traded for articles needed. Thus the presents were really not gifts at all but were actually loans.

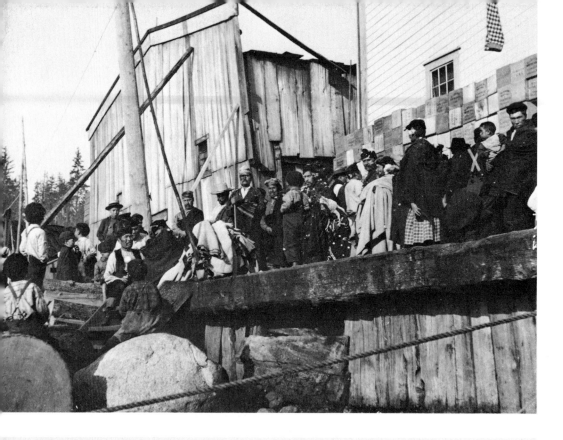

Photographs taken in 1901 (Alert Bay, British Columbia) show a Kwakiutl chief and his kinsmen awaiting their guests at a potlatch; a drummer beating a wooden box to call the guests while he sings a welcome song; the guest chiefs about to enter the house. Boxes of pilot crackers stacked against building at right are potlatch gifts. It was at about this time that the Indians lost interest in their carving.

During the first few days of the potlatch, the matter of the new totem pole and its raising was kept in closest secrecy. The newly carved treasure was carefully hidden in a place known only to the host and his trusted helpers. Finally, as the potlatch neared its end, the host chief called his guests together and told them it was time to raise the new totem.

Then, amidst laughter, shouting, rolling of drums, and general uproar, the helpers carried the red cedar log into the center of the applauding group. The hand clapping and the roll of the drums continued as the pole was dragged or carried near the hole dug for it. With many hands tugging at the ropes, the new pole, with the carved faces always turned toward the beach, was raised in all its glory. Once the earth was filled in around the base, dancers trampled the ground to make it firm. When the ropes used in the raising had been cut away, the handsome red cedar monument stood for all to admire.

The host chief, holding up his right hand and commanding the drums and applause to stop, came forward. It was his pleasant duty to explain exactly what the carved figures meant. He began at the top of the pole and moved downward.

In ending his speech, the chief called for the spirits to preserve the new pole and protect his people. This talk was usually followed by praise from the crowd for the host and his new totem. But such was not always the case, for at some pole-raisings envious guests were known to make insulting remarks about the pole and even the whole potlatch. In a few cases these words led to fights at once or even to small wars later.

When the pole-raising, the final and most exciting part of the potlatch, was finished, it was time for the guests to start home. Food and gifts were loaded into the canoes. The host chief was thanked and bidden farewell, and the guests departed.

On the deserted beach the new totem pole stood alone, its faces staring sternly out to sea. And the beautiful wilderness was quiet.

Totem pole at Old Kasaan faces out to sea.

All the old poles were disappearing.

VI
Saving the Totem Poles

A DISPLAY of twelve totem poles attracted a great deal of attention at the Chicago World's Fair in 1893. This was about the time that the Indians of the Northwestern Coast were beginning to lose interest in the poles, and were gradually ceasing to carve them. So the feeling grew, especially among historians and other persons interested in the arts, that an attempt should be made to protect existing totems. If this were not done, a magnificent art form would be lost forever.

As noted, a red cedar totem pole left standing in the open could be expected to last about the lifetime of a man. As long as new poles were being made to replace the old ones as they rotted away, there seemed to be little cause for concern, although some disagreed with that point of view. But when the Indians, with a few exceptions, stopped carving the poles about 1900, some action seemed necessary.

Vandals and name carvers already had destroyed or mutilated many of the best poles. At Ketchikan one of the most beautiful poles, made in 1884, had been disfigured by initial carvers. At Wrangell the famous One-Legged Fisherman pole was damaged, one of its wings hacked and one gone. Other examples of such neglect are not hard to find. Probably no pole made before 1875 is now standing, and only forty-four of the old poles may

The United States Forest Service protected the poles at Old Kasaan as well as it could when Congress failed to act to provide money for restoration (photos taken in the twenties and thirties).

be found in all of southeastern Alaska. The totem poles in British Columbia were treated in about the same way.

Along with rot and vandalism, fire was always a threat to the poles. No one knows how many totems were lost when high winds caused flames to spread from forests or nearby buildings. Some of the best poles ever carved were destroyed in fires at Wrangell, Old Kasaan, and Sitka.

In some cases, the Indians themselves willfully destroyed poles either by fire or disfigurement. The carvings were a reminder of a past they often wished to forget. The white man's way of living had been accepted. In one village, Indians burned all the poles since they were thought to cause disease. Some of the poles did contain human skeletons, but, again, the real reason for the destruction was a desire of the Indians at this time in history to forget their ancestors.

The poles were especially unprotected once the Indians left their townsites, as they often did, to live elsewhere. Vandals, usually white, were known to have used the poles as targets in gun practice.

Although it was small, some action to save the totems began in 1906, and shortly thereafter two national monuments—at Sitka and at Old Kasaan—were set up. Two methods were used to save the poles. Some were put in museums or other protected places out of the weather, while some were restored with stain and paint and erected again outdoors in public parks. However, restoration work suffered from a lack of money.

Wondering whether there was anything in Old Kasaan worth saving after a fire in 1915 had destroyed three Indian community houses and many good totems, the United States Congress asked the regional forester, Charles Flory, to investigate. In a long report in 1921, Flory listed the usual things that had happened to the poles—weather, vandalism, fire, abandonment, theft for sale to souvenir shops, and even use as gun targets and firewood. But, wrote Flory, as many of the existing poles as possible should be saved because of their historic and artistic value. He suggested that the poles at Old Kasaan be shipped to the Sitka National Monument for protection. Nothing was done because Congress did not allow any money for the project, so the Forest

Charles Flory, regional forester, in 1921 suggested plan for preserving the remaining poles.

Service protected the poles at Old Kasaan as well as it could. The Canadian government, however, began work on restoration of poles in British Columbia in 1925.

Interestingly, it was the relief program of the Great Depression of the early 1930's that brought about a restoration of some of the Alaskan poles. In 1934, a suggestion by Flory to use relief labor to collect, restore, and relocate the poles found favor, and a study of the program was begun. But it was not until 1938 that the preserving of the Alaskan poles got underway in earnest. This was the first major attempt to save large numbers of the Alaskan totems.

Since the poles were owned personally by various Indians, permission to remove and restore them had to be obtained. When possible, rotten parts were replaced with new wood. Then the whole pole was treated with stain and paint. Poles that were hopelessly rotted or otherwise badly damaged were copied. In no case were poles or parts of poles destroyed. The badly decayed ones were stored. Old Indian carvers, those who had learned totem-pole making from their fathers and grandfathers as long as sixty years earlier, taught the art to young Indians, who were eager to be instructed. While the work of repair was going on, many of the Indian legends the poles told were collected and published by a number of scholars. Assisting in the program to save the poles were the cities of Ketchikan, Wrangell, Sitka, and Juneau, and the Indian villages of New Kasaan, Hydaburg, and Klawock, all near Ketchikan.

From Old Kasaan the best poles that remained after the fire were taken to New Kasaan. An old Indian community house also was restored there. Poles obtained from nearby deserted villages were placed at Hydaburg, Klawock, Saxman, and Chief Shakes Island, the last near Wrangell. Not counting the work at Sitka,

Two views of Old Kasaan, (Above) before the fire of 1915, and (Below) before the removal of the remaining poles in 1970 for preservative treatment

forty-eight old poles were restored and seventy-three new poles were copied from the old ones.

But duplicated poles were considered fakes by the older Indians, who could not understand the white man's purpose in making new poles. Many of the Indians had no interest at all in the plan for saving the poles. "Why does the white man," they asked, "now wish to save the poles he at one time stopped the Indian from making?" They were referring to laws in certain places that had prohibited the holding of potlatches.

The beginning of World War II and the increasing employment due to defense jobs ended the relief program, and restoration of the poles lagged. Totem parks located within the Tongass National Forest in Alaska were kept up, but those controlled by communities outside the government areas usually were not protected. Tragically, for another twenty years, the dwindling supply of genuine old poles continued to be exposed to the weather and vandals.

It was not until the late 1960's that interest in saving the poles was revived. Then, in 1970, a plan was made in the new state of Alaska to remove all the poles that remained in native villages and place them in protected sites. It had taken more than sixty years for the advice of Charles Flory to be followed. Similar restoration work was being done about the same time in British Columbia, where many excellent poles, especially those of the Gitksan Indians, still stand. The Gitksan poles, while not skillfully carved, are among the tallest, ranging up to sixty feet in height.

Centers where restored poles may now be found in large numbers in the open include parks in Ketchikan and Sitka in Alaska and parks in Victoria, Vancouver, and Prince Rupert in British Columbia.

Totem poles at long last have become recognized as an art form. Although once important only to the people who made them, the totems now have appeal everywhere. Not all peoples did as well in keeping an artistic record of their history as the Indians of northwestern North America.

The mystery of the totem pole has a special attraction for the young artist, and many art teachers have found it easy to interest their pupils in the construction of a pole. Students have drawn totem poles with pencil, water color, and oil, developing their own symbolic meanings. Totems have been made from cardboard tubing, soap, clay, plaster, and cement. In real totem style, poles have been carved from balsa, spruce, poplar, soft maple, or any other good soft wood. Tools employed in classroom woodcarving include the hatchet, gouge, chisel, knives of various kinds —especially the drawknife, and old razor blades for the delicate work. Paints, varnishes, and shellacs are used sparingly on the poles, because the young artists remember that the old poles were only slightly decorated.

An art teacher in Alaska appropriately used the totem motif in her classes to make a pole which now stands outside the school building. School work "came to a screeching halt," said Kathryn J. Arend of the James C. Ryan Junior High School, Fairbanks, Alaska, "and students stared in disbelief when two men rolled a sixteen-foot spruce log into the art room. Sure, we had studied the designs of the Indian-carved totem of southeastern Alaska. We had run a contest selecting the best student design. Naturally we had talked about wood-carving techniques, but this was just too much. The students seemed to agree. It was impossible. How could a group of junior high students who had never held a chisel and a mallet carve a totem out of this huge, bark-covered hunk of wood? The answer was simple—a bit of

The totem pole carved by students in art classes at the James C. Ryan Junior High School, Fairbanks, Alaska

Students at the Maywood Avenue Elementary School, Maywood, New Jersey, work on totem poles as an art project.

planning, a little self-confidence, and a whole lot of hard work."

As the carving progressed, certain students emerged as experts. They directed the cutting. The teacher coordinated the work from one class period to the next. "As the carving progressed and the design took shape," the teacher continued, "the students developed pride in their individual contributions to the project." Interest spread throughout the school. Then someone "goofed," cutting the low figure on the pole too deep. But the error was corrected—at least partly—when a student carved a large fish and attached it to the damaged area. In due time the pole was painted, and later, with all the school looking on in a type of potlatch gathering, the pole was raised outside the school. It still stands there.

After having learned something about totem carving in his high school art class, Steven Greenquist of Galesburg, Illinois, carved a pole for the nearby town of Abingdon. Described as the tallest pole east of the Rocky Mountains, it depicts phases of American history, including the face of Chief Sakuwan, a famous totem Indian of British Columbia.

Totem poles have also been used effectively as advertising media. In an appeal for blood bank donations, one large life insurance company used a poster of a totem pole to convey the idea that the "entire tribe was covered." Thus the attractiveness of the totem pole as a means of expression continues today.

(Right) This excellent example of totem carving stands in Stanley Park, Vancouver, British Columbia, a symbol of the former days of glory of Coast Indian tribes.

(Far right) The totem pole used as an art motif in a poster for an area drive for voluntary blood donors. Posters were displayed in apartment communities owned by Metropolitan Life Insurance Company.

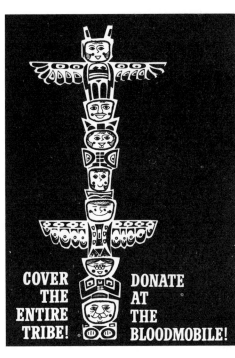

COVER
THE
ENTIRE
TRIBE!

DONATE
AT
THE
BLOODMOBILE!

Because of the growing interest in them, poles are still being restored and replaced. But the old poles really cannot be replaced once they are gone. This is because totem Indian life, with its mystery, no longer exists and is no longer understood. Carvers still make a few totem poles, but they cannot show a way of life they do not know.

Pronunciation Guide

Bella Coola	belluh'kooluh
Coast Salish	coast saý lish
Haida	hi'duh
Kwakiutl	quack eé oodle
Nootka	noót kaw
Quilliute	quill eé yoot
Tlingit	tooling git—in popular usage often klink it
Tsimsyan	chim sheé an

Bibliography

Annual Report of the Smithsonian Institution. Washington, D. C.: United States Government Printing Office, 1938-1939.

Arend, Kathryn J. "Totems Take Teamwork." *School Arts.* April, 1972 (71:30-32).

Barbeau, Marius. *Haida Carvers in Argillite.* Ottawa: National Museum of Canada, 1957.

———. *Totem Poles*, Vols. I and II. Ottawa: National Museum of Canada, 1957.

———. *Totem Poles of the Gitksan, Upper Skeena River, British Columbia.* Ottawa: F. A. Acland, 1929.

Barrow, Tui Terence. *Wood Sculpture of New Zealand.* Rutland, Vermont: E. Tuttle Company, 1964.

Brindze, Ruth. *The Story of the Totem Pole.* New York: Vanguard Press, 1951.

Clifford, Howard. *Much About Totems.* Seattle: Western Airlines, 1962.

Cooperative Agreement Between the State of Alaska, Alaska State Museum and the Forest Service. Washington, D. C.: United States Department of Agriculture, 1970.

Dorian, Edith, and W. N. Wilson. *Hokahey! American Indians Then and Now.* New York: McGraw-Hill, 1957.

Drew, F. W. M. *Totem Poles of Prince Rupert.* Prince Rupert, B. C.: F. W. M. Drew, 1969.

Feder, Norman. *North American Indian Art.* New York: Praeger Publishers, 1971.

Forest Service Work in the Preservation and Restoration of Totem Poles. Washington, D. C.: United States Department of Agriculture, 1971.

Garfield, Viola E., and Linn A. Forrest. *The Wolf and the Raven: Totem Poles of Southeastern Alaska.* Seattle: University of Washington Press, 1961.

Hofsinde, Robert. *Indians at Home.* New York: William Morrow and Company, 1964.

Keithahn, Edward L. *Monuments in Cedar.* Seattle: Superior Publishing Company, 1963.

Kuh, Katherine. "Alaska's Vanishing Art." *Saturday Review,* October 22, 1966 (50: 23-31).

La Farge, Oliver. *The American Indian.* New York: Golden Press, 1960.

Wherry, Joseph H. *The Totem Pole Indians.* New York: Wilfred Funk Company, 1964.

Index

About the Author

GLENN HOLDER, who was born in Indiana, was graduated from DePauw University, and earned a master's degree and a doctorate at Indiana University. He taught in the Richmond, Indiana, public schools, and became the director of secondary education there. At present on the faculty of Ball State University, where he teaches English, he has written or collaborated on eight books, mostly in the field of English language arts.

The author enjoys reading and gardening, when he is not teaching or writing. He is married, and he and his wife look forward to visits with their two sons and grandchildren during summer vacations.

It was while on a trip to Alaska in 1970 that Professor Holder became interested in the linguistic phase of totem poles, after examining one carefully at a totem park. "The thing fascinated me," he said. His research gradually led him into the writing of this book.

DATE DUE